A ROBIN'S
BOOK OF
GARDEN VERSE

Fresh, New Ways to Learn
about Britain's Favourite Bird

by **A Robin,** Esq.

In Memory

ISBN: 9798273622098
© A. Robin, Esq 2025.

Illustrated by Robert Stephen Parry

en–gb used throughout

CONTENTS

Introduction

Hello — and a pleasure it is, I'm sure, to make my acquaintance once again!

Now, if you've read any of my previous books — the Robin Almanac, for instance (2023), or the Magnificent British Garden Robin in His Own Words (2021), then you might find some of these little scraps of verse to be vaguely familiar. A few have been borrowed from those venerable pages. But don't despair. For seekers of value, be assured that numerous fresh items have been added.

There are also background notes to each of the poems, which are organised according to the seasons, and by which you can learn all about us robins and our mysterious ways. So, kind of educational at the same time. You'll find these towards the rear of the book.

There are some excellent illustrations again, in glorious black and white for those who enjoy colouring — and all produced by the same lucky chap I got to help me with the other books (I still reckon you've got to give these young hopefuls a chance, don't you?)

Anyway, before we begin, just a couple of questions I suspect you might be asking yourself as you contemplate whether to make this splendid book of verse your own. Firstly, the title. Why the book of 'Garden Verse?' Well, based on my observations over the years — I do live in a garden, after all — I've concluded that gardeners are not all that different to normal people. No, *really*. It's just that they happen to wear a lot of old clothes and don't go away on holiday all that often.

In other words, you don't have to be a gardener to enjoy these little observations in rhyme. They are for everyone.

The second question — and it's an important one, I'll grant you that — is why exactly should a book of verse pecked out by a robin in his spare time, be of any relevance, anyway? Well, let me mark your card! Robins, although small and lacking in education, are actually pretty smart ... *as birds go*. We are highly observant; immensely courageous and, no matter what the time of year, we sing every day, even when we don't need to. How's that for inspiration!

Robins, moreover, really do live on the edge, in constant peril and danger out here in the wild — there being so many creatures who simply want to eat us! Our lives are often quite short as a consequence — and there aren't all that many poets among us, either.

So, there you have it! For all these reasons and many more, I reckon you ought to be snapping up this little gem while you still have the chance. And then, when you're done, and if you can bear to part with it, you'll have the perfect gift to pass on to a special friend, if you have one — and space on your bookshelf, too, for the next robin masterpiece when it comes along

If there is one.

Observations
in Winter

A Robin's Book of Garden Verse

Legend

From the Robin Almanac

Robin Redbreast is my name,
Of noble legend and of fame.
For courage, I'm renowned and bold.
Yet when the weather turns to cold,
I come to sing beneath your gable,
For a tiny crumb from your kitchen table.

For context, see page 110

A Robin's Book of Garden Verse

Sleeping Arrangements

It's cold, cold, cold!
Especially for a robin who's old, old, old.

There's a gap in the wall of the garden shed.
And there inside I shall make my bed.

For context, see page 111

A Robin's Book of Garden Verse

Season's Greetings

From the Robin Almanac

At early morn, he greets you from the window
sill,
A scratching and a tapping and a voice so shrill.
And not just yet with any certain reason,
Comes robin with a blessing,
For the joyous festive season.

For context, see page 112

New Year's Blessing

From the Robin Diary 2025

The year to come is an open book,
Who knows what it will bring.
Robins always greet it boldly.
We like to dance and we *love* to sing.

The year ahead is a winding road,
Who knows where it will lead?
A fresh beginning, a clean blank slate.
May yours be blessed, and truly great!

For context, see page 113

A Robin's Book of Garden Verse

Wondering

Cats and hawks and foxes
They stalk and lie in wait
Biding time till a robin comes by,
But they're not searching for a mate.

Their jaws are cruel and strong,
They take a life, that theirs might flourish
And know not what they do is wrong,
But take us to their young to nourish.

I wonder what it's all about
This being born to die?
That we must live so much in doubt?
Or should we even wonder why?

There is no answer I can see,
But to greet each day, and just to *be*.
For a robin's life is not very long.
Just enough for a dance and a song.

For context, see page 114

Chums

From the Robin Almanac

You're never lonely in a garden with a robin,
When he comes up and greets you,
A-jumping and a-bobbin.

And if you share your lunch with him,
You'll have a friend for life.
Through thick and thin he'll be with you,
Through sadness and in strife.

For it's a universal truth,
On which you may depend,
That you'll always have chums,
If you've got a few crumbs.

For context, see page 115

RSP

Anticipation
From the Robin Almanac

When the weather is our enemy,
When the clouds tower high above,
Happy is the robin who bides his time,
Recalling days of nests and love.

For context, see page 116.

RSP

Vanquished in Battle

From the Robin Almanac

Young robin lies a bleeding,
No longer the strutting cock.
Vanquished and defeated,
It came as quite a shock.

Be sparing with your prattle,
Be humble in your might.
So when the chains of old age rattle,
You're sure to feel alright.

For context, see page 117

Old Cat Plodding

The plodding old cat is on the prowl.
So, is robin reckless,
When he seems not to care?
No, not at all.
Neither foolish nor feckless.
For it often does you good,
To indulge in a dare.

For context, see page 118

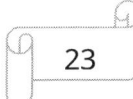

23

Liberty

From the Robin Almanac

Put not Robin in a cage.
It really will not do.
Robins need to fly, you see.
That's what robins do.

None can match our melody.
None can match our charm.
You find us in the garden, free,
The woods and parks and farm.

Outstanding in appearance,
Perfected in our call.
Put not Robin in a cage,
For liberty is all.

For context, see page 119

Winter Blues
From the Robin Almanac

So many hate the winter,
It really gets them down.
It makes them grim and miserable,
And all they do is frown.

But when they tell you life is pointless,
That's a funny kind of blindness.
For life is never pointless,
When you can show somebody kindness.

For context, see page 120.

Celebrations
of Spring

Loyalty
From the Robin Almanac

A robin lives for joy and romance,
He likes to sing, and he likes to dance.
Make for him a garden, and he'll love you too,
Forever, it's true.
(If you give him half a chance.)

For context, see page 122

A Robin's Book of Garden Verse

A Bench in the Shade

Everyone needs a bench in the shade,
Somewhere to go when you put down your
spade.
Where cool, gentle breezes come to your aid.
A place of repose in your own peaceful glade,
Or somewhere to chat with friends you have made.
You just can't beat it: a bench in the shade.

Everyone needs a bench in the shade,
To ponder design or mistakes you have made,
A place to rest when you've got in a muddle.
A handy little spot to shelter and huddle,
Or welcome a lover, to kiss and to cuddle.
The joys and temptations of a bench in the shade!

Everyone needs a bench in the shade,
To view all the work you have done and displayed,
A place of solace when memories fade,
Where echoes of laughter and happiness played.
No matter how far from home you have strayed,
You'll always return to your bench in the shade.

For context, see page 123

34

Celebrations of Spring

RSP

On Being Small

Why, the gardener asks,
  Should roses have thorns?
They are so sharp and spiteful.
For such fair, noble, beauteous plants,
Maintaining them is simply frightful!

But robins do not mind the thorns,
For we are only small,
Thus, we can weave ourselves between,
And not get hurt at all.

For context, see page 124

A Robin's Book of Garden Verse

Skylark

From the Robin Almanac

If I, a robin, could a skylark be,
I would take me high up to the sky,
And all the world below me I would see,
And happy, I would be,
Just to fly, and fly, and fly.

(Perhaps it's like that when we die.)

For context, see page 125

39

Unaccountable Urges

L ove, Love, love, I say!
It makes a robin's brave heart sing,
  Just to be alive today
In the fresh, green heart of spring.

For context, see page 126

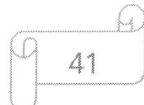

At it Again!
From the Robin Almanac

Beware, other robin,
You shall not come near.
Not while I'm busy in March,
Do you hear!

I shall sing my resistance,
If you don't keep your distance.
And never, my friend, shall you see me at rest,
Till I've pecked you and chased you,
From this place I have blessed.

For context, see page 128

A Robin's Book of Garden Verse

A Little Something
From the Robin Almanac

In May, I come a-courting
With a little something in my beak,
To give to my fair robin love,
Who likes to chirp and cheep.

I hope she won't be coy or giggly,
When I bring her something nice and wriggly.
In May I come a-courting
With a little something in my beak.

For context, see page 129

Choices

The world we know is a garden,
It brings us all our needs.
It's up to us to tend it well,
Not let it run to trash and weeds.

Best not to waste the time we have,
Or view the work as chores.
But celebrate each precious day,
And the garden that is yours

For context, see page 131.

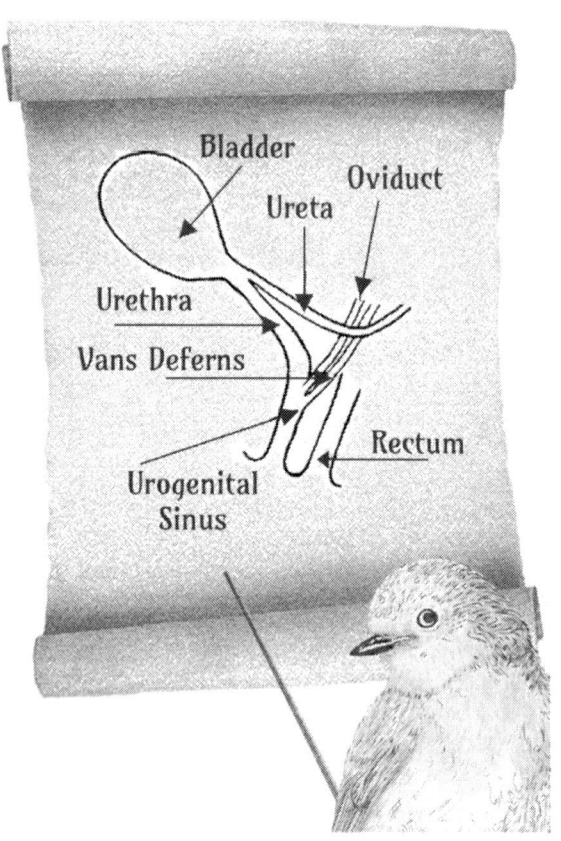

Facts of Life

Most birds have a cloaca.
It's a funny sort of name,
But eggs and 'body functions'
All exit from the same.

It opens to the outside,
Here beneath our tummies,
And it's just the same for daddies,
And it's just the same for mummies.

I know it might sound odd to you,
But see it from our angle:
There's nothing to obstruct our flight.
Nothing that can dangle

An organ that is versatile
And meets our needs completely
We do not have to make a fuss,
But manage things ... discreetly

For context, see page 132

49

Robin in the Oak

I really like the robin down the road.
She sings from the oak tree, That's her abode.
   In winter, I used to chase her away,
But now I think I'd like her to stay.
It's strange to suddenly feel this way,
For the robin in the oak.

It's like we have a destiny,
A song composed in harmony,
That henceforth we shall live as one
And even have a bit of fun.
It's love, when all is said and done,
For the robin in the oak.

I'd like to fetch her something tasty,
(I'll think it through, I won't be hasty.)
Not a slug, a wasp or a bee,
But a dainty spider from the tree.
I hope she likes the look of me,
The robin in the oak.

No matter what the seasons bring,
We'll face it with delight, and sing.
We shall not turn in dread, or flee
From all the dangers that we see,
And only death will ever separate me,
From the robin in the oak.

For context, see page 133

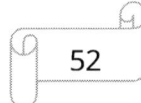

Plans

From the Robin Almanac

The April showers pay tribute to the glade,
They make the bright flowers dance and shine,

And a bonny nest with babes shall be made,
If only she will consent to be mine.

For context, see page 134

Dawn Chorus

From the Robin Almanac

At dawn, there's such a terrible din,
With all the other birds joining in.
I can hardly make myself heard.
Noisy, noisy, noisy bird!

For context, see page 135

A Robin's Book of Garden Verse

Stoic Robin

From the Robin Almanac

Now is the season of danger,
From fox, and hawk and cat.
Our babes have so many foes,
Threats and hurts from this and that.

A robin's life is short, it's true,
But that is nature's way.
Fear, thus, no more the fox or hawk,
Than the passing of a day.

For context, see page 136

Kissed by Moonlight
From the Magnificent British Garden Robin

At night, I wake
With stars in the sky,
And sit with Endymion,
As the Moon sails by.

For context, see page 137.

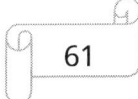

A Summer's Gothic

He looked at me, the sparrow hawk
With those horrible, murderous eyes.
A bird, I should remind you,
Ten times a robin size,
And with a nest of hungry babes.

He came up close, the sparrow hawk.
I said, listen, can we talk?
I think I know just how you feel
But I'd rather not finish up as a meal,
For your nest of hungry babes.

I, too, have chicks a-needing (I said),
Without me they will want of feeding,
And starve, they will without my care,
Should my misfortune take me there
To your nest of hungry babes.

Be not disturbed, the hawk declared,
I've only come to say hello.
It's not when you see me you should be scared,
But when in flight, unseen, I swoop below,
And know you little of the ending.

Today, you're young and quickly moving,
Alert and strong and sleek,
And should I fail it would be tiresome proving.
I go instead for the old and the weak,
For my nest of hungry babes.

Thus, time alone is all you have to fear.
For we shall meet again, no doubt, next year.

For context, see page 138

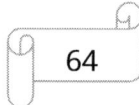

Expressions of Summer

A Robin's Book of Garden Verse

Inseparable
From the Magnificent British Garden Robin

No one knows
And no one sees.
At dusk we come,
To bathe our little robin knees.

For context, see page 139

Nest

From the Robin Almanac

When the nest is full of young,
And we work with tireless pleasure,
We know one day they will depart,
And memories be our treasure.

For context, see page 140

Slugs

Slugs, slugs, slugs.
On a night-time quest to decimate,
So cold and slimy, soft and weak.
You'd have to be quite desperate,
To put one in your beak.

Slugs, slugs, slugs.
So very many, hardly rare!
Bold and cheeky, almost tame,
And gardeners, who quite despair,
Rightly treat them as fair game

Slugs, slugs, slugs.
Never wanted, never cherished,
They're back again the very next day,
Descendants of the ones who perished,
Munching the lettuce and strawberries away.

Slugs, slugs, slugs.
No two alike, yet all the same.
You have to say, they are resourceful,
It's just a shame, a crying shame,
They taste so ruddy awful!

For context, see page 141

Expressions
of Summer

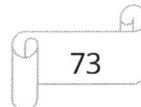

The Weather Forecast

It's mighty hot again today
And hot tomorrow, so they say,
  Those clever birds with their weather sums,
Predicting when the summer comes.

For context, see page 142

A Garden for the Birds

Do not disdain your garden weeds.
They multiply so fast, indeed!
You cut them down and pull them out
Without a care, regret or doubt.
And sometimes greet them with a curse,
And cry, there can be nothing worse!

Yet most of us are weeds to God,
Not that special, not that odd.
We strive each day to find a place
To cultivate our humble race.
And are forgiven if we stray,
That even we might see the light of day.

Why strain to bring about extinction
Of plants that simply lack distinction?
Just find a place to make a border,
And keep a few in tidy order.
(You may, of course, control the rest,
Just keep the ones that you like best.)

Weeds are useful, please have a care,
They grew in peace long before you were there.
For here might bees and insects go,
Birds and wildlife thrive and grow.
And thus shall you be granted pardon,
When next you step into your garden.

For context, see page 143

Expressions of Summer

A Robin's Book of Garden Verse

Humble Robin

From the Robin Almanac

When summer's plenty sets us free,
In the bounty of leaf and fern,
Wise birds will humble be,
And think on fortune's wheel,
That does not cease to turn.

For context, see page 145

Meditations
On Autumn

What to do about the Fledglings?

I think I always liked them best,
As little robins in their nest.
For now they're out and so much older,
They seems so proud, so brash and bolder.

Spotty-feathered fledgling things!
That never hunt and never sing.
We fetch and bring them all they need,
While they just sit around all day and feed.

It's not that we don't fret or care,
But if they sometimes were not there
We wouldn't be upset or sad (no really!)
We might, in fact, be rather glad.

That they might flourish, learn and grow,
Perhaps it's time to let them go.

For context, see page 146

A Robin's Book of Garden Verse

Special Remedy

Little ant, please don't protest,
I'd like to hold you in my beak.
I know you do not like it best.
I hear you grumble, hear you squeak.

You spray some kind of toxic thing,
When you are in distress,
So I shall trail you through my wing,
Then hold you to my breast.

The fleas and bugs don't like it,
And neither do the lice.
It stings a bit for me at first
But then becomes *quite nice.*

Oh, tiny ant, I thank you so!
You helped me out so much today,
That now I'll gladly let you go,
And watch you turn and run away.

For context, see page 147

The Moult

There's always a time,
For old feathers to go.
A time to renew,
A time just to grow.

There's always a moment
To let go of fear,
To let go of doubting,
To listen, and to hear.

And always a moment
To wish yourself well,
And treasure this world,
Where you happen to dwell.

For context, see page 149

Decisions

From the Robin almanac

The time is nigh
When a robin must decide,
Whether to flee,
Or else to abide.

Foreign climes will beckon us,
With promises galore.
But boldly facing winter's storms,
Is just as brave, I'm sure.

For context, see page 150

91

Pride of Vest

From the Robin Almanac

What do you think of my new scarlet vest?
I reckon it's better than all of the rest.
It came when all my old feathers fell out.
And now I'm ready to sing and to shout.

For context, see page 151

93

A Robin's Book of Garden Verse

A Robin's Lament

I remember she who once sang so fine,
Until one day she gave her song to me.
For off she went to sit upon the nest she'd made,
In silence, for what seemed an eternity.

And then the eggs of a sudden hatched.
Astonishing as the tiny beaks broke through,
And all so fast, like in a batch.
And all so many — not just a few!

Then life was never quite the same again,
As we hunted together for food,
Back and forth through wind and rain,
Feeding and raising our tiny brood.

Until one day she fell to the floor.
Just scattered feathers on the ground.
Not a whimper, not a sound.
A hawk had been; she was no more.

So now I perch upon our tree,
And make each day my loudest trill.
Defiant, proud and singing still,
For she who gave her song to me.

For context, see page 152

Youthful and Reckless

Don't migrate this year, they say,
It's really far too risky.
Staying here's a far better way,
And the cold will keep you strong and frisky.

That's what the other birds do.

Well, I don't care what the other birds do!
I don't care what the other birds say!
I'm a brave young robin through and through,
And I'll fly where I will, and I'll do what I do.

Toodaloo!

For context, see page 153

Grim Times

From the Robin Almanac

Grim times, when summer's joys are fled.
It can make a robin sad.
Bleak and darkling, full of dread.
But it need not be so bad.

For if you're sad or gloomy,
Here's what you can do:
Admit that there is sadness, yes.
But the sadness isn't *you*.

For context, see page 154

Comfort Eating
From the Robin Almanac

The robin I loved has flown away,
I hope she'll survive to return some day.
Until that comes, I shall wait patiently,
And eat up all those berries
On the old Holly tree.

For context, see page 155

Goth Robin
From the Robin Almanac

By ancient ruins, ivy-clad,
Sings Robin Redbreast at close of day.
Perched on bough in dusky gloom.
And neither joyful nor yet sad,
Caught in the splendour of a bright crimson ray.

For context, see page 156

The Final Song

Sweet Robin sings in the autumn.
Sweet Robin sings in the fall.
Sweet Robin sings at the close of the day.
Goodbye, farewell,
That's all.

For context, see page 157.

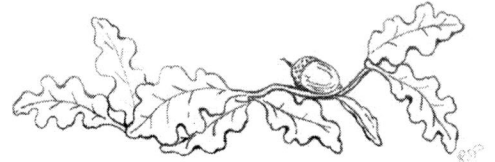

Each of the Poems
in Context

Legend

From page 7

Robins are not only Britain's favourite bird, but we have also been famed and rightly adored throughout most of British history for our resilience, our cheeky familiarity and our good looks. We quite rightly enjoy legendary status.

Yet as individuals, we are only mortal, and we need to eat. In winter, especially during harsh conditions, there can be very little available, so we have to humble ourselves occasionally. We have to put ourselves about, so people can notice us and — hopefully — feed us.

So you are honoured, that we come to you in our hour of need — that a creature so proud and handsome has asked you for help. A few crumbs will do — and for a robin, it cheers the heart and can mean the difference between life and death.

Be kind and generous, therefore. Don't let us down!

Sleeping Arrangements

From page 9

Robins are pretty good at finding places to sleep. We organise ourselves to be safe and not to be attacked in the night by creatures like foxes or badgers. We also do our best to keep out of the wind and the worst of any driving rain. But when the really cold weather strikes, we are not averse to entering outbuildings for shelter. Sheds, garages, barns — anything to help us get through the long winter nights.

So if you have a shed, for instance, with a few likely robin-sized entrance points, try to refrain from repairs until the warmer weather arrives. We vacate any building with first light, and won't return until dusk. So check during the day to see if you can find any evidence of our occupation — the odd little spec of white droppings, for example.

In the spring, we might also use a shed or barn for nesting. And then you will certainly know we are about, as the nest of straw and old leaves should be obvious. Please leave well alone if you see this. The female robin might even be quietly sitting on her nest, incubating her eggs and hoping to remain invisible.

Season's Greetings

From page 11

Just why we robins have come to be associated so closely with Christmas is a long story. You'll find a thorough exploration of this topic in my book 'The Magnificent British Garden Robin' — but suffice to say it has a lot to do with uniforms and Victorian postmen.

Anyway, we really don't have any objections to this connection, and in fact robins rather approve of it, since it means that folks who perhaps wouldn't normally bother with the existence of small garden birds, start to pay us special attention at this time of the year — and, perhaps if we're lucky, be more likely to feed us.

A word of caution here, however: please don't offer us samples of Christmas specialities like pudding or mince pies because these might well contain alcohol, and even a little of this can be damaging to our health.

Bless you!

New Year's Blessing

From page 13

Following closely after Christmas is, of course, New Year's Eve. It's a time when humans naturally look forward to a fresh start. Robins, too, are eternal optimists, and even though the dates on your calendars don't really mean much to us out here in the wild, we do sometimes sense your excitement.

This is especially the case when you frighten us half to death by letting off fireworks on New Year's Eve or go about making a terrible din in the middle of the night, just when we're trying to get some sleep.

Nevertheless, we wish you well.

Wondering

From page 15

Imagine that every night when you go to sleep, you fear you might be eaten up by some monstrous predator and never see the light of day again. For robins, this is a constant possibility. Badgers, foxes and rodents can all pose a threat.

The daylight hours are scarcely any less fraught with danger — for then we have the sparrow hawks, kestrels and cats to contend with.

For our youngsters, it is even more precarious. Fledglings just out of the nest are scarcely aware of their vulnerability, but the very process of survival into something approaching maturity depends on it. We have to learn fast — to be on our guard at all times.

Yes, it can seem unfair. The more thoughtful and philosophical of our species might even get to wondering why this should be, at all? Are we here just to feed and nourish other creatures — or is there a measure of pleasure and satisfaction we can take from our short lives?

Chums

From page 17

There are one or two peculiar and fanciful ideas surrounding robins. That robins appear when a loved one (a deceased one) is near and such like. Well ... clever people who study wildlife and nature will tell you that's not possible. But, just for the record, I would like to suggest that you should probably not be so sure of yourselves in this respect.

But no matter. Your typical British robin is certainly near when you have something they want. For example, they like to follow a person who goes about digging in the garden and raking up leaves and things because it reminds us of the days when, in the wild, we would follow wild boar or badgers about in the woods to pick up whatever wriggly items were left behind. For modern-day robins, gardeners are just like that.

Best of all, however, is if you have a few crumbs of tasty food to share with us. Then you will definitely have a friend, a feathered one in this instance, and one who is perfectly willing to become a loved one when near.

Anticipation

From page 19

Unlike most humans, a robin will have the opportunity to raise several families of young during its lifetime. We can even complete this joyous task two or even three times in any given year.

As many an astute gardener knows: 'for everything there is a season'. And robins, being often very wise, instinctively know that there are moments for action and moments for simply biding one's time and doing nothing.

We know that winter is not suitable for us to be rushing around building nests and raising chicks. It's a waste of vital energy. The weather is harsh; the hours of daylight short, and there is only a limited supply of food on the ground for us to gather. And believe me: young robin chicks demand *a lot* of feeding.

So, in winter, we think of the good times. We recall them, treasure the memories, and wait.

Vanquished in Battle

From page 21

Robins are fiercely territorial, and they can begin establishing and defending their territory as early as the turn of the new year, when the days lengthen — and certainly will be busy doing so in earnest come the spring.

Unfortunately, the problem with occupying a good patch of land with a nice garden and plenty of food, is that there's always going to be another robin somewhere who wants a piece of it. And that really won't do.

However, I'm glad to say that most disputes over turf can be settled peacefully through a series of specific measures, from singing loudly to bold, aggressive posturing. But when the issue cannot be resolved this way, actual fighting can ensue. This can become extremely violent if neither party chooses to give way, and can result in injury or — rarely — even in the death of one of the combatants.

A combination of humility and a willingness to compromise is often the wisest choice in many instances — and not just for robins. But some birds simply have to learn the hard way.

Old Cat Plodding

From page 23

Robins can be mischievous sometimes — in fact, *most of the time* when cats are concerned. Young, well-camouflaged cats are a menace, of course. And you have to show them respect. But an old house cat out for a stroll is fair game.

We like to hop around in front of it and make a real nuisance of ourselves, leading it a merry dance all around the garden, tiring it out before it even gets a chance to pounce.

Wicked, aren't we!

Liberty

From page 25

Believe it or not, it was once common (until quite recently, in fact) to see wild birds kept in cages. People enjoyed their beauty and their song. But of all the birds subjected to this dreadful custom, the robin has always been the most unsuitable

What a waste! What a travesty, that so many of our most magnificent and most beguiling characteristics should be curtailed and repressed by a state of captivity! Beauty can never be enhanced by confinement — nor by those who would hold it captive for their own transient enjoyment.

A robin's character is one of intense independence. We don't go about in groups or gather together for any kind of common purpose, as many other species of birds do. And although you can tame us to a degree, even to the extent of having us eat out of your hand, we will always have our boundaries. We need to be free.

So long live robins, I say! And long live liberty for all creatures!

Winter Blues

From page 27

This poem is an observation on creatures who make themselves miserable just because the weather is a bit gloomy.

It might be said that kindness is the key to overcoming self-indulgence. And robins believe in kindness. Apart from certain dubious old traditions of robins covering the eyes of the dead with leaves, there are more reliable observations that demonstrate how we put this philosophy into practice.

For instance, if one of a nesting pair of robins has the misfortune to be bereaved through predation, it is not unknown for another robin to step in as surrogate 'aunty' or 'uncle' to the young brood. This, you might argue, is easy when there is an abundance of food available in the summer months, and it does aid in the overall survival of the robin species. But here's another story to demonstrate the kindness of robins.

Once upon a time, in the depth of winter, I noticed a little mouse, who strolled up and down a certain regular track by a hedge, searching for whatever meagre items of nourishment might be available. The mouse was obviously in distress and starving.

Now, the chap that manages my garden, and who has his house in it as well, is in the habit of putting out crumbs for me, and quite a generous amount. So I took a nice piece of bread in my beak and flew over to the spot I knew the mouse would visit. Then I left it there for the little fellow to find.

So there you are! And if you don't believe me, just ask that chap who takes care of my garden. He saw it happen.

Loyalty

From page 31

This poem is all about mutual benefits. A kind of symbiotic relationship, as clever people might call it. Let me explain ...

You love your robins — of course you do! We are amazing creatures: adventurous, courageous, and incredibly good looking — and yet, I like to think inherently modest and unassuming at the same time (*ahem!*).

But did you know that robins love you too? Or they *can* do, if you play your cards right. My book The Magnificent British Garden Robin outlines our terms in this respect. Provide a peaceful garden with plenty of shelter and places to forage; somewhere to bathe safely and perhaps a nesting box placed discreetly, and you'll find us loyal and loving — and in return we will have no objections whatsoever to you watching us and admiring us every day.

How's that for a bargain!

A Bench in the Shade

From Page 33

Robins love a nice perch. Just take a look at all those Christmas cards with cute little red-breasted birds sitting on fork handles, branches or walls. And what could be better for a bird or a human alike than a comfy bench in the garden available for a moment's repose? Not that we robins have too much time for repose or idleness — since we have to keep hunting for food, needing to consume around a quarter of our body weight each day just to stay alive (that's my excuse, anyway).

No matter. Even robins need a breather every once in a while. And of course, yes, a bench is a handy spot to meet your special robin friend, as well, when the breeding season comes along.

Thanks to gardeners everywhere for providing us with a bench in the shade.

.

On Being Small

From page 37

Sometimes being small and nimble is an advantage. Rose bushes usually contain lots of little flies and grubs to eat, and we can reach inside the bushes easily and pick them off. Providing the gardener hasn't sprayed them with some obnoxious chemical, that is — as some gardeners seem compelled to do with roses.

Actually, watching the gardeners this time of the year is quite amusing. Not only do they insist on treasuring their delicate roses, and bearing all the sorrows of disease and blackfly that blight them, but they insist on training them over arches and pergolas, just those places where they have to pass through or beneath, making for a lot of torn clothes and bandaged fingers.

Funny lot, those gardeners.

Encourage your ladybirds if you want to control the blackfly, and birds will take care of the caterpillars.

Very tasty.

Skylark

From page 39

Few birds can match the skylark in spectacular demonstrations of flight — though usually flight in one very obvious direction, straight upwards, accompanied by a melodious rhythmic call that has been celebrated by writers and composers over the centuries. Its song as it rises has forever been associated with the delight of an English summer. The metronome of timelessness.

The ascending flight and song of the skylark is actually an elaborate mating ritual. It demonstrates the strength and vigour of the male to any female watching in awe. At least, we must assume she is watching.

So high can the lark climb that the world below must appear very different to that ever achieved by a songbird like me, who can only look on at such feats of aeronautical mastery, and listen in wonder as the song gradually fades from our hearing, the higher and higher it extends. If angels exist, then this is surely as close as most creatures can come to imagining their scope and range of vision.

Unaccountable Urges

From page 41

Springtime is the season of delight for robins. After conserving our energies and struggling to keep body and soul together through all the harsh winter months, we are at last free to get cracking on the all-important business of mating. All this sweeps us along pretty quickly into the commencement of courting; building a nest; laying eggs and raising a family of little robins as they hatch and take their first stumbling steps into the world.

The changes can happen very quickly, almost overnight — not just the irrepressible urge to find a partner, but also the various physical changes that take place inside, as well, to accompany it.

They say, for example, that the testes of a male robin, which are internal, will increase in size by as much as a thousand-fold at this time.

What do you think of that? If something similar happened to you overnight, fellas, you'd soon make a song and dance about it, wouldn't you!

Not only that, but the very world around us changes too, with everything growing and bursting into colour and song, flooding the garden in bright, luminous colours that simply were not there a few weeks earlier. It all chimes in and resonates perfectly with the extraordinary transformation taking place within.

Imagine — just imagine! It's amazing, the changes in the way we feel.

And we just love it.

At it Again!

From page 43

Male robins will not tolerate other robins nearby at this time of the year — apart from our chosen partner, that is. So passionate and assertive do we become defending our territory that we can fight to the death against intruders. After all, this is springtime. We have been waiting all through the winter for this opportunity. There is no way of predicting how many chances we will get to breed, so this is all suddenly very serious.

Consolidating our own territory is vital, therefore. It ensures the male has access to an ample supply of food both for the female while she is sitting on the nest, and for all the robin chicks that will shortly hatch and demand to be fed as they grow.

That's why you'll see us pouting and strutting in a kind of war dance much of the time, and even leaping up into the air at moments to show off our magnificent scarlet chest to any rivals nearby.

If all this fails to make an impression, then we will fight, clawing and pecking until our foe is vanquished or we ourselves perish. No quarter given.

A Little Something

From page 45

Courtship feeding is common among many species of animals and birds. It serves the purpose of bonding between a pair. With robins, however, it becomes elevated to a fine romantic art form.

Yes, all right, I know the idea of being presented with a wriggly caterpillar or spider to eat is not exactly to everyone's taste or expectations of courtship, but for robins it's all we have available if we are seeking to impress. And we really do wish to impress, more than anything in the world at this time. There is also a method to the madness, since with the prospect of several eggs to be laid and then incubated, the female needs a little extra nourishment at this stage in the breeding cycle.

It is the male of the robin species who gathers the morsel of food and who does the giving, and the female who receives the gift. Never the other way around. It is the most important aspect of lovemaking for us.

The female becomes so excited upon being presented with this token that she flutters her wings and chirps and cheeps in delight.

It's wonderful. And the actual act of union that may or may not follow afterwards, is not really all that significant to either of us. It's the food that counts. (I understand that some humans are also likewise inclined.)

Choices

From page 47

Gardens are places of abundance and pleasure, or they can be if a little care is taken to cultivate the bounties of nature.

It might well be true that you can gain an insight into the character of folks by the way they regard their outdoor spaces, and especially their gardens.

This is because the garden within is every bit as important as the one we see around us.

And robins, who often experience short and difficult lives out here in the wild, have long since concluded that there is no use worrying about things if life is not entirely perfect. We just have to make the best of it and face each day with courage.

In other words, it's up to everyone to choose the best, and to cultivate what we are given with love and pride.

Facts of Life

From page 49

If your garden robin's method of procreation is a mystery to you, then you will find a clear and thorough explanation in my book The Magnificent British Garden Robin, where I explain exactly how it takes place.

Suffice to say that birds are not at all constructed the way humans are. Our sexual organs are hidden, or internalised. We have a tube-like opening to the outside, both male and female, called the Cloaca, and everything — eggs, sperm, ovaries and so on — all connect to it and function through it.

Because of this, there is, in fact, no outward indication as to whether a robin is male or female, and — despite what you might hear from certain unverified sources — there are no tell-tale signs in plumage or markings either that can distinguish between us.

Some humans might well envy this arrangement of our most intimate anatomy. It certainly is a most practical and discreet way to go about things and to celebrate equality between the sexes.

Robin in the Oak

From page 51

A robin pair are so devoted to each other during the season of mating that it might well be fair to say we become as one. It all happens so suddenly and so powerfully that we cannot really imagine life without the presence of the other. It's like some great classic of romantic literature taking place in all the gardens up and down the country during the spring and summer. (a bit like the Cathy and Heathcliff of the robin world).

What is so ironic about it all is that just a few short weeks prior to this, we might well have been at loggerheads, fighting each other to establish territory — because, believe me, female robins can fight just as fiercely and ruthlessly as males.

And then, without warning, almost overnight, it all changes. Romance ensues, and then there is just no stopping us.

Indeed, at the height of our relationship, it seems that only the death of one or the other can ever separate us. And it only comes to a conclusion in the autumn, after a successful brood of chicks has been raised and they have gained their independence.

Plans

From Page 53

Male robins really only have a one-track mind at this stage of the year. Will our wooing be well received? Will our gifts be appreciated? Will our favoured female consider us suitable? Are we handsome enough, strong enough, reliable enough? And will we get together and make babies?

Those are our plans, and nothing else matters much.

After all, this is exactly what we've been struggling for all through the winter — to stay alive and get ourselves ready for this one fabulous moment of destiny. It really is that important, so please help us out a little if you can.

How? Well, a strategically placed nest box is a good way to start. Put it up securely as early as you can, and long before we actually need it. That way, we will not feel suspicious or anxious about making it our home for a few vitally important weeks. Thank you very much. Then let us alone to get on with things. That is perhaps more important than anything. In other words, don't pry. Don't fuss.

Do not disturb!

Dawn Chorus

From page 57

The period of the exultant dawn chorus of birds all singing loudly together in early summer mornings is a wonderful phenomenon. There is good reason for it, naturally. It's to consolidate our nesting territory. But we are all of us in celebratory mood, anyway, right now — pretty much at the height of our powers and enjoying the prospect of long, productive days feeding our young and just doing what we enjoy the most.

Robins love the sound of their own voices, of course, their own melodious singing — for which we are rightly famed. And it can be so frustrating to be overwhelmed and drowned out by such a racket!

Stoic Robin

From page 59

What with so many horrid predators lurking about — hawks and foxes (not to mention domestic cats) robins have to be more alert and cautious now than ever. The worst of it is that, at this time of the year, our little robin chicks become so terribly exposed, especially when they finally *fledge* and leave the nest. For the first few days out, their flight feathers are not properly formed, and they tend to stumble about and hop rather than fly properly. So they are very vulnerable.

And so are we, because we are so concerned and focused on their safety, occupied with feeding them still (they will expect to be fed for many more days yet, if not weeks!).

There is, of course, no sense in worrying about it. If a robin spends its life worrying about death, nothing would ever get done by way of living.

For us, death is an inevitable prospect: nature's way. And we learn to be philosophical about it (as philosophical as a robin's brain can ever be, that is). We come to regard our ending no more than we would the passing of a day.

Kissed by Moonlight

From page 61

On rare occasions, robins are heard to sing at night — rather like the nightingale (though not anywhere near as beautiful as that famous songster of the poets).

Bright urban lights often keep us awake and active, and a bright full moon can sometimes make our sleep shallow. Moonlight is also a significant aid in those times when some of us choose to migrate overseas — as some robins do in the autumn.

So we are, occasionally, observers of the Moon — a bit like the mythological shepherd, Endymion, who was visited each night by the amorous moon Goddess, Selene..

Thus, certain robins of a romantic disposition (most robins are incurable romantics) will happily allow themselves to wake on the short summer evenings and be kissed by moonbeams.

A Summer's Gothic

From page 63

Of all the predators a robin must fear, the sparrow hawk is arguably the most dreaded of all. During the summer months, these airborne monsters are especially active, having their own nests of chicks to feed — and robins are certainly on the menu.

The only advantage a robin has by means of survival is its own alertness; its youthful intelligence and a willingness to keep track of what is perched nearby or moving about in the sky — since the hawk's favoured mode of attack is by swooping down at incredible speed to impact their prey and kill them. The robin is then dismembered on the spot, its innards torn out and the pieces taken away.

Our own young fledglings, although fairly alert, are far too trustful and unfortunately not very bright. So they often get picked off, along with any older or weaker robins. So, as you can imagine, the declining years are not exactly an enticing prospect either.

Inseparable

From page 67

Robins are some of the most hygienic of birds. We like to bathe regularly, at least once per day. It helps to keep our feathers in good order and aids us in the essential process of preening — that is, using our beaks to maintain and to properly align our plumage. We use a spot of natural oil from a special gland near the base of our tails for this — and a little moisture on our feathers helps, too, in this respect.

So if you wish to attract robins to your garden, investing in a suitable birdbath is probably the best thing you can do. We really enjoy bathing, and if you have a birdbath in your garden, you'll often see us lingering and splashing about in it long after any necessity for cleanliness or preening is complete.

We prefer to do this at dusk, because it is safer. And sometimes a mating pair will even hop in together, splashing about blissfully in the fading light.

Our little luxury.

Nest

From page 69

The breeding cycle proceeds apace during summer– far more quickly than we could have imagined or even wanted. Once the fledglings have been out of the nest a few days, they become almost independent. They can fly a little, and we struggle to locate them sometimes — though an exchange of special cheeping sounds between us is usually enough to discover where they are.

It's a bit sad, really, the inevitability of it all — and that they will go their own way eventually and no longer need us. A funny feeling. I believe you call it 'the empty nest syndrome'.

These very same little birds might even one day come to regard us, their own parents, as rivals for this very same territory.

Cocky little so-and-so's.

How's that for gratitude!

Slugs

From page 71

For most gardeners, especially those seeking to grow fruit or veg, little explanation is necessary for this item of verse.

Slugs are pretty amazing creatures, actually. They clean up much of the debris in the garden overnight, and their anatomy is extraordinary. They have eyes on stalks, and have thousands of tiny teeth somewhere (has anyone ever counted them?)

To try and control the slug population is, of course, futile. And we robins find it quite amusing watching gardeners fuss and fret as they seek to apply all manner of ingenious remedies to the situation — some quite gruesome.

Best solution of all, is to foster a thriving population of slug predators, such as frogs and toads, hedgehogs and birds. Robins are not all that keen on slugs, unfortunately, but some birds find them quite acceptable.

No accounting for taste.

The Weather Forecast

From page 75

Robins are clever at predicting the weather. We have to be. It's vital to be able to forecast the direction of the wind, for example, and also the possibility of this altering during the course of a long winter's night. That way, we choose the best spot for sleeping and for staying safe.

Migration is another topic that requires a degree of prediction. And we are pretty good at that, too, choosing the best time to leave and, perhaps even the best route to reach our destination safely. It just comes naturally to us, without really understanding how.

We do appreciate that folks can become very preoccupied with the weather, as well – expending lots of energy and resources on forecasting what's to come. But robins simply observe and know. They will raise the equivalent of one ironic robin eyebrow at all the fuss, and then move on.

A Garden for the Birds

From page 77

I hope this doesn't come as too much of a shock, but birds are really quite fond of weeds. They might not be all that beautiful to some folks, but for us they are wonderful places to forage. The larger clumps, moreover, like briars and other prickly undergrowth, can even offer protection from predators at night when we sleep.

Someone once described a weed as being simply a flower in the wrong place. It's all about attitude. And you can learn to like them. A tidy border around almost anything can make things look good, too — like a picture frame around even the most indifferent of paintings.

The decision to go for a wildlife garden as opposed to a cultivated, orderly plot, is not always an easy one, I know, and won't be to everyone's liking. There are other people you share your home and garden with who might disapprove of the policy – not to mention the neighbours! In that case, you can go for a partial wildlife garden. Try adopting a little wild and weedy patch somewhere out of the way. That would be a good place to start.

Just make sure to remove the weeds before their seeds spread everywhere — though even these, if left, will provide sustenance to wildlife. Birds, mice and voles will eat the seeds before most get a chance to germinate.

An organic, robin-friendly garden usually takes care of itself, in other words. You can find lots of tips and ideas in my 'Robin Almanac' — including a monthly list of jobs not to be doing in the garden, month by month.

Try it and you'll feel much more relaxed about things, I promise, and might even learn to love your weeds a little, too.

Humble Robin

From page 81

At this time of the year, when Mrs Robin might be sitting on a second batch of eggs for hours on end, and I am up here on our tree singing all day to keep our plot secure, there's lots of time to think.

Now, I'm not sure thinking is always a good thing. There are lots of folks who get themselves into a terrible state by thinking too much. But anyway, I decided that it might not be a bad thing to be realistic and humble, that everything in life moves in cycles, and just when you are on top of the world and everything is going your way, it might not be a bad idea to consider that change is inevitable. The wheel of fortune that crops up in so many folk tales and ancient wisdom teaches us that.

So be humble, I say. Count your blessings and prepare for change. Because it always comes, no matter how much we wish it wouldn't.

In other words, I won't be getting all upset when autumn starts to show up. I'll be ready, knowing I've made the best of the good times..

And I'll be content.

What to do about the Fledglings

From page 85

Once they have been out of the nest for a few weeks, the young robins should be finding their feet and seeking a measure of independence. They conceal themselves in the undergrowth much of the time, and their spotty-brown plumage helps in this respect. But they will be sporting their first conspicuous red feathers on their chests soon — a sign they are becoming quite adult.

Unfortunately, we, as parents, sometimes become a little impatient. After all, we have worked hard all summer long, perhaps raising two or — in some instances — even three families of robins. Autumn is here now, and we are tired.

Added to that, we have the dreaded moult upon us at this time of the year, when many of our most important feathers simply fall out, to be gradually replaced with new ones. It's good when it's all over, but you feel wretched while it's taking place. So the last thing we need right now is a lot of temperamental 'teenage' robins moping about.

Yes ... even robins can become a bit grumpy at times.

Special Remedy

From page 87

Well, this is a bit personal, but I'll let you into a secret. Robins, like most birds, tend to suffer from a somewhat embarrassing condition in the hot weather. It plagues us during the summer months, and when we get a warm 'Indian summer' in the early autumn, it's somehow even worse.

What happens is that we get some little visitors who aren't at all keen to leave — namely fleas, mites and lice. They all seem to want to take up residence in our feathers or attach themselves to our skin. It itches like mad!

Bathing helps a little, but never seems to solve the problem entirely.

Fortunately, there is a special remedy on hand, namely ants. Yes, ants! You see, when they are in distress, as you might imagine an ant would be if it were picked up in a bird's beak, they emit a chemical — formic acid — I think you call it.

And this stuff is brilliant. While the ant struggles, we direct it carefully to all the right spots, and it kills the bugs and lice — or at the very least encourages them to go elsewhere.

The procedure itself, *Anting*, as it's called, can even be become quite addictive – and our relief is so great by the time we're finished that we don't even eat the ant afterwards, but let it go back to all its mates and tell the unlikely tale.

Fair exchange, I reckon.

The Moult

From page 89

Birds and their feathers: it's an intimate relationship. We can't just change them like you do with your clothes, when you put on a new jumper and wash out the old one to use again. Our feathers just wear out after a time and have to be discarded before being replaced by new ones.

It's an annual event around late summer into autumn, and the old ones have to fall out first before new ones can grow, and that takes time.

They don't all go at once. It's a process that proceeds by stages in an orderly fashion so, for example, we are never entirely without some of those all-important flight feathers on our wings. We do try, however, to keep a low profile during this period, so you might find yourself wondering where exactly we have vanished to.

But what a relief when it's over! There is something oddly satisfying about it, too — about letting go of the past. A bit like being reborn.

Decisions

From page 91

Autumn is a period in which some robins decide to migrate. They fly from the UK to places like the south of France or Portugal, an enormously long journey undertaken usually at night for safety. They go with the expectation of returning in the new year, and it is often the female robins who go, with many of the males staying behind to face the winter and defend their territory.

So ... am I going to be reckless and fly off, too? The way I see it is that bravery is not just about travelling miles to a foreign shore just to live it up in the sunshine. Bravery is also about facing the difficult times at home. It will be challenging, of course. I know that. The snow is the worst — when you can't forage for food at all. And the nights are very long and very cold. Decisions, decisions.

The younger robins, of course, have no qualms about migrating if they want to. They just fly off! But what about me? And perhaps it's too late to go now, anyway?

And even if I did go, would I be able to regain my territory when I return? Would I be strong enough?

What would you do?

Pride of Vest

From page 93

So, now the moult is over, and robins can get back to doing what robins do best — that is, showing off and strutting their stuff.

If you happen to see us out and about, don't forget to compliment us on our radiant new appearance.

(You might not really have noticed the difference, but just pretend.)

A Robin's Lament

From page 95

Out here in the wild, tragedy can strike at any time, and it's almost inevitable that at some stage a robin will lose its mate.

The female robin tends to relinquish her singing during the nesting period. Obviously, she would not wish to draw attention to her location at such a time. It's dangerous enough as it is, and her eggs are sometimes damaged or eaten by other birds or rodents on those occasions when she leaves the nest, even for a few moments.

The male robin, on the other hand, takes over the singing with even more enthusiasm than before. It's as if the female has given her song over to him for a while.

Robins do actually sing all year round. Unlike other birds, we really never stop. And there is a certain noble defiance about that, don't you think?

We might be small, but we never surrender to the harsh world we are born into. And we never allow misfortune to silence us.

Youthful and Reckless

From page 99

So, as we have seen, at this time of the year, each robin has to consider his or her options very carefully. To fly off to warmer climes and risk all the dangers of the journey there and back, or to stay put and endure the rigours of a typical British winter, which is fraught with its own dangers, of course — not least of which are the spectres of starvation or freezing to death.

Well ... migration really is a great adventure, I suppose, especially if you are a young and, dare I suggest it, *reckless* robin.

For them, it's best not to listen to what the other birds are saying. Especially the older ones. Far too cautious.

Grim Times

From page 101

Robins can feel a bit despondent at moments. Is it the prospect of winter looming? Will we get through it this year? Will we survive? Or is this *it* — the final winter of all for some of us?

The trick is to parcel up all that doubt and sadness and put it to one side. We do not allow ourselves to be defined by sadness. We are independent of it, and strong.

True freedom.

Comfort Eating

From page 103

Like many creatures in the wild, a robin has to fatten up at this time of the year — either to fuel migration or else to see it through the cold weather at home, coming soon.

And, anyway, if your former mate has taken it upon herself to whizz off overseas, I reckon it provides a robin with the perfect excuse to indulge a little, don't you?

Goth Robin

From page 105

In our hearts, robins appreciate our history, that we are in essence of an ancient heritage, and that our behaviour and spirit possess an almost Gothic elegance and mystery. Sunset and autumn, old buildings and gnarled trees — these are the natural haunts in which to display ourselves.

And, as you know, we do like a bit of display.

So, when the clouds part and we face the setting sun on a golden autumnal evening, we know deep inside, and you know it too, that we are, in the most time-honoured and special way, really quite magnificent.

And perfect.

The Final Song

From page 107

Because robins sing every day, and especially keenly around dusk, it is only inevitable that there will come a time when we will be singing our final song. And if we fail to wake the next morning, we will have ended well, don't you think?

So we will sing, and continue to sing to the close of the final day as we have lived from the very first — as one tiny spark of a greater light that shines forever in the darkness: Britain's favourite bird.

Index of First Lines

Index of First Lines

Index of Topics and Themes

You might find this list helpful if you require a piece of robin verse or a garden-themed poem for a special occasion or speech.
Topics are listed in no particular order.

Topics and Themes

Other Books by A. Robin, Esq..

A.Robin, Esq. has produced two previous books designed to help folks understand and look after garden robins in the UK. They are both illustrated and make ideal gifts for anyone interested in nature and wildlife in the garden — and, of course, robin welfare especially.
Available in paperback and hardcover.

Here they are ...

THE MAGNIFICENT BRITISH GARDEN ROBIN — IN HIS OWN WORDS

Why are robins such friendly birds? What exactly do they like to eat? And where do they build their nests? Is the robin's reputation for promiscuity at all justified? And do they really sing because they're happy? Entertaining, informative and forthright. The ultimate guide — in his own words — to one of Britain's most cherished garden residents

THE ROBIN ALMANAC

Robins and their gardeners rely on an instinctive understanding of the cycle of the seasons. Now, for the first time, an almanac has been compiled by the celebrated Avian writer A.Robin, Esq. — providing, in his own words, valuable information on robin behaviour, how to maintain a suitable wildlife habitat, and jobs not to be doing in the garden, month by month.

Printed in Great Britain
by Amazon

a24da931-ebc1-48b6-b215-bfdb1584bc66R01